HARRIS COUNTY PUBLIC LIBRARY
3 4028 08733 8209

W9-AUU-801

JOSEPH MIDTHUN   SAMUEL HITI

BUILDING BLOCKS OF SCIENCE

ANIMAL LIFE CYCLES

WORLD
BOOK

a Scott Fetzer company
Chicago
www.worldbook.com

World Book, Inc.
233 N. Michigan Avenue, Suite 2000
Chicago, IL 60601
U.S.A.

For information about other World Book publications,
visit our website at www.worldbook.com
or call 1-800-WORLDBK (967-5325).
For information about sales to schools and libraries,
call 1-800-975-3250 (United States),
or 1-800-837-5365 (Canada).

Library of Congress Cataloging-in-Publication Data
Animal life cycles.
     pages cm. -- (Building blocks of science)
  Summary: "A graphic nonfiction volume that
introduces various animal life cycles, including birds,
amphibians, butterflies, and mammals"-- Provided by
publisher.
  Includes index.
  ISBN 978-0-7166-2824-8
  1. Animal life cycles--Juvenile literature. I. World
Book, Inc.
  QL49.A5846 2014
  571.8'1--dc23
                              2014004654

Building Blocks of Science, Set 2
ISBN: 978-0-7166-2820-0 (set, hc.)

Printed in China by PrintWORKS Global
Services, Shenzhen, Guangdong
1st printing July 2014

Acknowledgments:
Created by Samuel Hiti and Joseph Midthun
Art by Samuel Hiti
Text by Joseph Midthun
Special thanks to Syril McNally

TABLE OF CONTENTS

There is a glossary on page 30. Terms defined in the glossary are in type **that looks like this** on their first appearance.

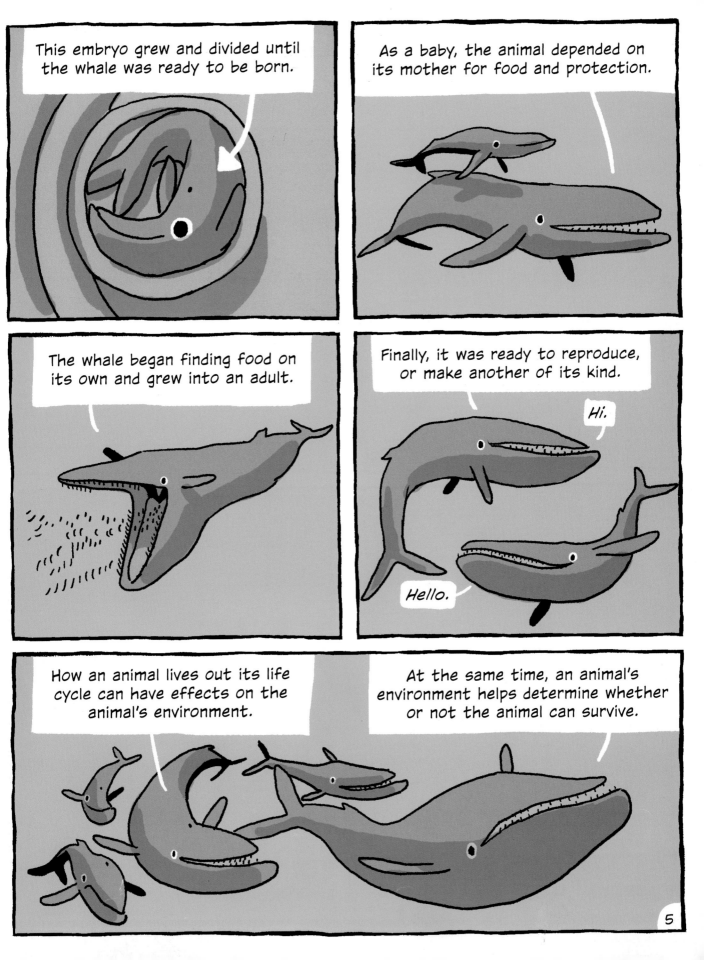

The male makes special cells for reproduction called **sperm** cells.

The female makes special reproductive cells called **egg** cells.

Plants can also reproduce sexually through a process called pollination.

Some plants and animals can reproduce **asexually,** meaning by themselves.

Boing

Without reproduction of any kind, living things would die off completely.

Among birds, **mammals**, reptiles, and most animals on land, a few eggs are fertilized inside the female's body.

Because the eggs are protected inside of the female's body, they are more likely to survive and be born.

Plop

However, when this chicken gives birth, it will produce not another chicken—

—but an egg!

Let's take a closer look at some animals that lay eggs containing their offspring.

PoP

9

EGGS AND OFFSPRING

Similar to how a sunflower seed has the potential to grow into an adult sunflower, an animal egg has the potential to grow into an adult of the same kind of animal.

Both cranes and alligators lay eggs on land.

These types of eggs have tough or leathery shells.

They hold a large amount of nutrients that are contained along with an embryo within a watertight shell.

Both animals' shells also hold in moisture so the eggs will not dry out on land.

The alligator offspring grows inside the shell, developing into a miniature adult, and eventually uses up all of the nutrients.

One day, the offspring is ready to break free from its protective shell.

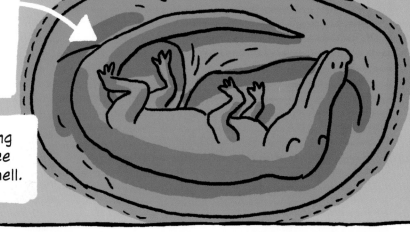

The eggs of most birds have a similar shape, but vary in color and size.

Most eggs laid in sheltered nests or holes in the ground are white.

Most eggs laid in uncovered nests have protective coloring.

The eggs of this duck are shades of brown.

They blend right in with the cattails and reeds.

Nearly all mammals develop their young from eggs inside of the body.

After a growing period, the mammal gives birth to live offspring.

PARENTAL CARE

Most amphibians, fish, and reptiles provide little or no care for their young.

They usually have many offspring because most will not survive to adulthood.

Are we there yet?

Other animals, like this kangaroo, provide more care.

They usually have fewer offspring because most will survive.

The baby kangaroo, or joey, is carried around in its mother's pouch until it is ready to run and hop on its own.

Most birds sit on top of their eggs to keep them warm.

After the eggs hatch, the parents bring the chicks food, like worms, small insects, or even small mammals, until the chicks can fly.

For instance, crabs molt, or shed, their outer shell covering and grow larger adult bodies.

POP

1   2   3   4

Other animals may lose their baby teeth or grow new adult fur.

Hey, I lost a tooth!

Penguin chicks grow thick coats of feathers to keep warm.

That's right!

Cheetahs grow from a cub to an adult by becoming physically stronger.

Cheetah cubs are kept safe by their mothers and learn the skills needed to hunt as an adult.

METAMORPHOSIS AND THE AMPHIBIAN

Many young animals look much like their adult parents.

A puppy looks like an adult dog, except that it is smaller.

Other animals go through incredible changes as they grow up, or mature.

For example, frog eggs will hatch into tadpoles.

Tadpoles are not like adult frogs.

In the animal kingdom, a common threat to an animal's life span is **predation.**

BUZZ

Predators are animals that naturally hunt, kill, or eat other animals—

Snatch

—their **prey.**

Predator animals are almost always **carnivores,** or meat-eaters.

Prey animals are commonly **herbivores,** or plant-eaters.

?

In the wild, a coyote is a predator.

A hare, if it is not fast enough—

—might be its prey.

LIFE CYCLE DISRUPTIONS

When wild animals die much younger than their expected life span, it is called a **life cycle disruption.**

This can happen to any organism, including predators.

Disruptions in animal life cycles can be caused by food shortages, **invasive species,** diseases, habitat destruction, lack of water, pollution, and even tiny **parasites.**

Humans are a direct cause of life cycle disruption in both animals and plants.

As **omnivores,** many humans survive on a balanced diet of animals and plants.

But, humans can also cause indirect disruptions to the organisms in their environment.

Sometimes domesticated, or trained, animals are kept by humans as pets.

LICK LICK

But, sometimes, a pet can be reintroduced into the wild as a stray by escaping or by being abandoned.

Burp

Despite life cycle disruptions, certain jellyfish and other creatures have the ability to grow and change in a way that makes them seem to "live forever."

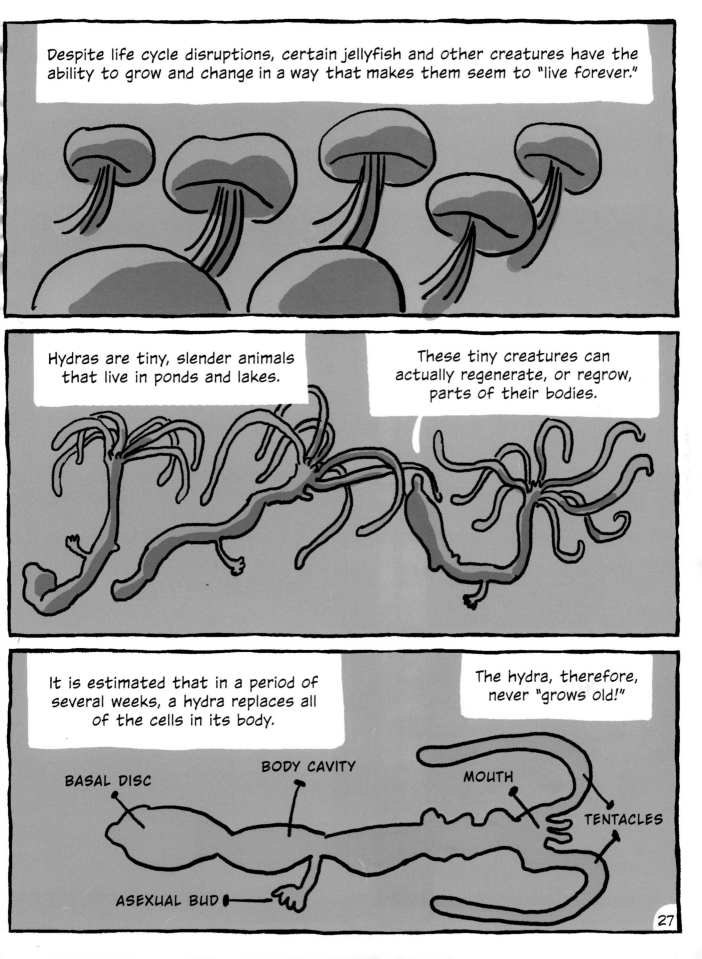

Hydras are tiny, slender animals that live in ponds and lakes.

These tiny creatures can actually regenerate, or regrow, parts of their bodies.

It is estimated that in a period of several weeks, a hydra replaces all of the cells in its body.

The hydra, therefore, never "grows old!"

BODY CAVITY

BASAL DISC

MOUTH

TENTACLES

ASEXUAL BUD

GLOSSARY

asexual reproduction the process by which an organism produces an offspring without sperm cells or egg cells.

carnivore an animal that feeds on other animals.

chrysalis the hard outer shell that holds a pupa as it develops into a butterfly.

egg the reproductive cell produced by females.

embryo an animal or human in the early stages of its development, just after fertilization.

fertilization the process by which a male sperm cell and a female egg cell join together.

herbivore an animal that feeds on plants.

invasive species a nonnative species that moves into a new area and replaces the native species.

larva; larvae an active, young form of an animal before it goes through metamorphosis; more than one larva.

life cycle the stages that a living thing goes through as it develops.

life cycle disruption an unexpected shortening of an organism's life span.

life history the sequence of changes through which an organism passes during its lifetime.

life span the measure of how long an organism typically lives in the wild.

mammal a type of animal that has a backbone, grows hair, and feeds its young on the mother's milk.

metamorphosis the transformation of an animal from an immature form to an adult form.

offspring the young of an organism.

omnivore an animal that feeds on plants and other animals.

organism any living thing.

parasite a living thing that benefits at the expense of another organism.

predation when one organism eats another.

predator an animal that hunts and feeds on other animals.

prey an animal that is hunted by other animals for food.

pupa the inactive state of an animal going though metamorphosis.

reproduction the way living things make more of their own kind.

sexual reproduction the process by which organisms produce offspring with sperm cells and egg cells.

sperm the reproductive cell produced by males.

FIND OUT MORE

Books

Animal Life Cycles
by Sally Morgan
(Smart Apple Media, 2012)

A Dragonfly's Life
by Ellen Lawrence
(Bearport, 2012)

Food Chains
by Carol S. Surges
(ABDO, 2014)

Frogs!
by Laurence Pringle and Meryl Henderson
(Boyds Mills Press, 2012)

The Life Cycle of Mammals
by Susan H. Gray
(Heinemann Library, 2012)

Life Cycles: Grassland
by Sean Callery
(Kingfisher, 2012)

The Life Cycles of Butterflies: From Egg to Maturity, a Visual Guide to 23 Common Garden Butterflies
by Judy Burris and Wayne Richards
(Storey Publishing, 2006)

Step-by-Step Experiments with Life Cycles
by Katie Marsico and Bob Ostrom
(The Childs World, 2012)

Websites

BBC Bitesize Science: Food Chains
http://www.bbc.co.uk/bitesize/ks3/science/organisms_behaviour_health/food_chains/activity/
View an animated video explaining photosynthesis, predator-prey relationships, and how they work together in a food chain.

BBC Nature: Animals
http://www.bbc.co.uk/nature/animals
Watch thousands of short nature videos that identify and discuss hundreds of species of animals.

BBC Nature: Animal and Plant Adaptations and Behaviours
http://www.bbc.co.uk/nature/adaptations
Examine key topics about animal life cycles in short units, complete with topic introductions and wildlife video examples.

Centre of the Cell: One Cell Made You
http://www.centreofthecell.org/centre/?page_id=22
Take an in-depth look at the human life cycle and learn how your body was made from one tiny cell!

National Geographic: Red-Eyed Tree Frog's Life Cycle
http://video.nationalgeographic.com/video/frog_greentree_lifecycle
Watch a red tree frog move through its full life cycle—from a small egg to a mature adult!

National Geographic Education: Monarch Butterfly Life Cycle and Migration
http://education.nationalgeographic.com/education/activity/monarch-butterfly-life-cycle-and-migration/
How does a caterpillar transform into a butterfly? Find out by completing this step-by-step activity, with bonus downloadable worksheets.

National Geographic Kids: Creature Features
http://kids.nationalgeographic.com/kids/animals/creaturefeature/
Select an animal to watch a video or hear its call, or read an article to learn more about its unique characteristics.

INDEX